# "ESTABLISHED" TOPICAL BIBLE

## Christian T. Howell Sr

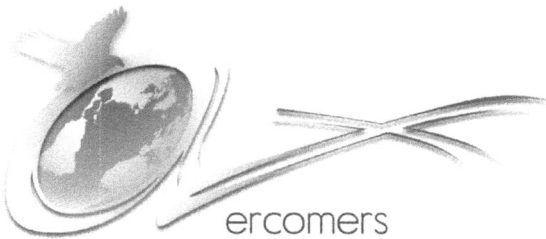

ercomers

ISBN:  978-1-7337342-3-3 (Paperback)

First printing, 2020

Christian Howell Sr.
P.O. Box 247
Riverview, FL 33568

www.overcomersmovement.org

Established is a word that is often used but rarely used in its proper context. Most times, when we hear the word used by others, we often think in terms having a large following or being successful. The dictionary defines *established* as successful for a long period of time and widely known or growing or flourishing successfully. The root word of established is *establish*, and it means to make firm or stable, to bring into existence, to put on a firm basis, or to put (someone or something) in a position, role, etc., that will last for a long time. Other less thought of meanings of the word include to prove or to put beyond doubt or to cause someone or something to be widely known and accepted. The formal definitions of the word broaden our understanding to include measurement of time. A key element to determine whether a thing or person is established is by measuring how long it lasts. The world may measure something by how quick it is built or by how fast it grows, but the true measuring stick of something or someone being established is the length of time that it exists.

In our culture, we often think in terms of a business, a dream, or an idea when we consider something as being established. But more than an entity, God wants His people and His name to be established. He is concerned and dedicated to our, yours and mine, stability and being established. Our being established in the earth reminds all of creation, and all of the enemy's forces that God and His Kingdom is established forever! A good visual analogy to use when thinking about established is that of a tree.

Trees can be planted at an early age, and even transplanted while it is early in its development cycle. The tree gets planted and develops roots that enable it to grow strong and endure environmental and human factors over the years. The main goal of planting and maintaining the tree is so that it adds value to the property and lasts for generations to come! As a matter of fact, trees are mentioned more in the bible than any other thing, next to God and humans. One of the most famous passage is that we are like a tree planted by the rivers of water that bear fruit (Psalms 1:3). That's an excellent representation of what it looks like when we say *established*.

The ultimate and epitome of being established rests in the Kingdom of God. Throughout the entire bible, it is the cornerstone of theology; it is the glue and stitch that ties the entire bible together. His Kingdom being chief, established, and enduring is the focus of the writings. Other than God being a Father, He is declared to be a King. And the consummate description is that He is King of Kings! The Old Testament prophets declared that there would be no end to His Kingdom and that all other kingdoms would be returned to Him. The New Testament declares that kings and kingdoms will pass away…but not the Kingdom that God establishes!

When we gravitate towards the mind of Christ, we start understanding the plans and purposes of God for our lives…and our family's lives. His original idea and blueprint was to make a leader of a family and their name great, and then to perpetuate that greatness generationally. "And I will make of thee a great nation, and I will bless thee, and make thy name great; and thou shalt be a blessing", Genesis 12:2. God's decree to Abram was about being established, not just to be secure or about being big or famous, it was about greatness and stability that was to last longer than he would be alive on the earth.

When the scriptures make reference to being established, there are a few words that it uses to fully express and define the word. In the Old Testament, there are more than 2,700 references to being established. The words used the most include "qum" and "yashab". Those two Hebrew words alone provide definitions of to arise, to set, to dwell, to remain, and to endure. The other Old Testament words in their original text includes the definitions of to stand up, to be firm or stable, to stand, to support, or to appoint.

In the New Testament, the two primary words used are "histemi" and "sterizo". Together, they alone are used more than 160 times in the scriptures. Their definitions include to cause to stand, to make stable, to place firmly, to fix, or to strengthen. Other meanings of the word in the New Testament include to set or place in a balance, to abide, covenant, to confirm, or to render something or someone constant.

Since the Bible compares and makes analogies to people and trees, we can definitely conclude that God is not interested in destroying, harming, and punishing people, He is always in the business of settling and setting people into long-term systems and processes of success. His primary concern is not about the speed at which something happens, but how correct it is built and ultimately how long it will last. With every plan that God creates, the enemy always has a counter, an adversarial plan, or a strategy to cause you and I to miss the blessing and benefit of being established. The enemy's masterplan is call instability…or being unstable.

Being unstable is a condition that is not easily defined, but it would involve constantly changing or shifting, being reckless, unbridled, or uncontrolled. Instability is the main reason and factor that relationships aren't long-term or successful. It is at the core or those in poverty despair, whether it surfaces in career or financial failures. When Jacob we preparing to depart the earth, he called his sons together to pronounce a blessing over them and to declare their future to them. Interestingly enough, he told his firstborn Reuben that because of his being unstable, he would not be able to prosper or excel. Can you imagine being told that your outlook on your future was directly tied to your whether you were established or not? But that's exactly the point – being established is critical to success in the Kingdom.

It is an important truth to understand that what God creates, He establishes! It is our job to maintain and fight for our stability, but God gives and grants it. This principle is found and settled in Deuteronomy 8:18, "But thou shalt remember the LORD thy God: for it is he that giveth thee power to get wealth, that he may establish his covenant which he sware unto thy fathers, as it is this day." He is establishing His covenant, and He's giving everything that's needed to get it done! It is the will of God for you to be established.

One of our most beloved scriptures amongst my peers and co-laborers is 2 Chronicles 20:20. It states "And they rose early in the morning, and went forth into the wilderness of Tekoa: and as they went forth, Jehoshaphat stood and said, Hear me, O Judah, and ye inhabitants of Jerusalem; Believe in the LORD your God, so shall ye be established; believe his prophets, so shall ye prosper" (KJV). A decent word study of that scripture reveals great truth that I'd like to explore with you for a moment.

In the latter part of the verse, the word believe and established are the same word in the original Hebrew text. That word is "âman". That word means to build up, to support, or to be firm, faithful, or permanent. When we apply the original meaning to the passage in context, it literally states that "if we are built up, firm, consistent, and permanently rooted in God, then we will truly be built up, firm, and consistent in the Earth. He supports us AS we support Him. When we get firmly planted in Him, He firmly plants us in the Earth.

Listen my friend, there is no real lasting success or prosperity outside of Him. As a matter of fact, the scripture in proper context says that we have to get established in Him BEFORE we ever encounter the kind of prosperity that we believe He intends for us to have. The correct order is: get established first, then prosperity second. OF what an answer to prayer that is to many believers. It gives assurance that your level of success isn't always a direct result of your work ethic or diligence, but it is always connected to your right relationship with Him.

Now let's give further context to the content concerning the verse we just explored. This passage is squeezed in between a crisis situation. They were being pursued by 3 larger forces and had run out of solutions and strength. They were at a place where the only thing that they had left was to try to keep their focus on God. (v. 12). When faced with this turmoil that seemingly was insurmountable, they received instruction to stand still and watch God do His work. This is where it gets good, in my opinion.

It's evident that their nation was gripped with fear because it is recorded to fear not numerous times in this setting. In the book of Psalms, it is recorded over and over that David said "in my prosperity (security, silence, peace), I said that I will never be moved" Psalms 30:6. In Psalms 66:2, he said "He alone is my rock and my salvation; He is my fortress, I will never be shaken". The point that I am trying to get across is that when in God, we have a peace during storms, a calmness during calamity, and a firmness when others are crumbling. We are established in Him.

The answer to the problem is hidden in plain sight in verse 17. The words "set yourself" and "stand still" share the same origin of being established. The instruction that they were given was that in the midst of an impending calamity, don't be easily moved…dig deep and be established. Don't panic, don't allow yourself to become overstimulated into too much activity, don't retreat…just settle into God and follow His instructions and all will be well.

This book is written at the beginning of a new decade…2020. I believe that the number twenty is a number that is directly tied to the principle of being established. Before you dismiss this, follow carefully. According to Genesis 26, Genesis 27, Exodus 36 and Exodus 38 the walls (support) and foundation were measured by twenty. Those who were required to give offerings and assist in the building process were measured by the age of 20.

When Israel established its army, the starting age was for those who were twenty and above. It took King Solomon twenty years to build the temple (God's house) and his own house, according to 1 Kings chapters 6 and 9. Also, do you remember when the ark of the covenant was allowed to be taken from Israel? It was gone for twenty years. There are numerous other scriptures that could be given to support and prove this truth, but suffice it to say that the number 20 definitely represents a time of being established.

We could also delve centuries forward into our own culture and realize that the last decade of the 20s were called the "Roaring Twenties". It was a time marked by great settling and growth. World War I had just ended and America had to be rebuilt. The economic and social climates were totally devastated, and change was needed and imminent. The roaring twenties was marked by great innovation, rebuilding, and a great time of getting established again as a nation. Jazz was born and became a norm,

For the first time in years, the economy became stable. People settled more in cities instead of living on farms. The dependence on automobiles was established and woman were given their permanent right to vote. The great migration from the southerners moving to the north occurred, and a new culture of music and dance stood up. It was the beginning of the Harlem Renaissance. Unmistakably, the 1920s brought into many new norms that are still evident in our culture today – it was a great decade of being established.

I believe that the decade of 2020 will be no different. 1920 started with a president ending a war and shifting the attention from foreign entanglements to economic growth. Just as it was then, so it is now in America. We are on the verge of breakthrough technological advancements that will forever change how we interact as humans. Make no mistake about it, we are embarking on new norms and cultural shifts. After a great tragedy, the world will evolve and new ways of life will emerge that although built upon an earlier foundation, will redefine our daily lives.

Before we look at the scriptures, I want to make sure that I emphasize that being established always means being grounded, set, and fixed firmly in truth. "Jesus saith unto him, I am the way, the truth, and the life: no man cometh unto the Father, but by me" John 14:6. Let's agree that Jesus is considered the Truth. His words are truth and His words are the absolute measuring stick for all truth. With that being said, the Apostle Peter declared that it is of utmost importance that we always be established in "present truth" (2 Peter 1:12). What I'm saying is this, being established carries a responsibility to keep our spirit rooted in what we "know about God", but also to realize that there is so much that we don't know that we cannot afford to ever stop learning.

My prayer, and sincere desire, is that while you are reading this book, making the confessions over your life, and meditating on the scriptures given, God will settle, ground, and establish you in every area of your life, and for generations to come. I pray that the truth of God's Word challenges and confronts every lie that's been released into your life and causes you to conform into the Image of Jesus Christ. I pray that because you accept and believe in Him, that He will establish you spiritually, physically, mentally, and emotionally – and that you will make better choices and investments that will follow you into eternity.

***This is does not contain an all-inclusive list of scriptures concerning being established.

# Confessions Over My Life

I give the Word first place in my life. I make my schedule around Your Word! Your Word is Truth and forever settled in Heaven; therefore, I establish Your Word upon this Earth. Your Word is a lamp to my feet and a light to my path. It is quick and powerful and sharper than a two-edged sword. I have hidden Your Word in my heart that I might not sin against You. I plant the Incorruptible Seed of Your Word in my heart. It is abiding in my spirit, growing in me mightily, and producing Your nature in my life.

The mountain of the Lord's house is established and exalted, in the top of the mountains and above all hills; all nations are flowing unto it.

I am the righteousness of God in Christ Jesus; therefore, I am established. I am like a tree planted by rivers of water. It is always my harvest season.

Every decree that I make, Lord, let it be according to your Word and let it be established in the earth now.

As a man thinks in his heart, so is he; therefore, my thoughts produce life and stability. My thoughts create solutions and wealth that impacts three and four of my generations to come.

Because I meditate on Your Word, my thoughts are established and are pleasing to You.

I commit my works unto the Lord; therefore, my thoughts are established and fruitful.

My emotions are balanced and stable. I am not easily moved by the opinions of man or unfavorable situations. I am established in my course of life.

The works of my hands, the things that I produce, are established.

I am established financially. I lend and not borrow. I prosper and advance in the marketplace as a trendsetter and as an industry disrupter.

All of the promises of God are active, effective, and established in my life and in my family's life.

God gives me massive and unprecedented wealth so that his covenant is evident and established.

Because I fear the Lord, my seed is great and mighty in the earth and wealth and riches are in my house. I fear no evil because I am grounded in the fear of the Lord.

I am established in righteousness. I am far from oppression, fear, and terror. They do not come near me.

God freely gives me spiritual gifts and I am confirmed and established as a child of God.

I am established in Truth. My discernment and judgment are accurate and unbiased.

I am free from all bondage and baggage tied to old truths, old rules, outdated models and systems. I am established in present truth.

I renounce and come out of agreement with every lie I have heard or believed concerning my life or concerning my bloodline.

I repent and renounce all double-mindedness and agreements or decisions that I made while unstable. I trust You more than I trust myself. Therefore, my heart is free from confusion, cares, and fatigue.

I bind and cast out every strongman that keeps my soul from being stable. I repent, cast out, and release myself from fear, anger, rejection, hurt, and every soul tie that opposes me being established.

I bind and come out of agreement with all spirits and assignments of arrested development that causes me to not grow and mature; attempting to leave me unstable.

Lord, free me from every unstable person or system that war against or disrupt my stability.

# OLD
# TESTAMENT

# GENESIS

Genesis 6:18 But with thee will I establish my covenant; and thou shalt come into the ark, thou, and thy sons, and thy wife, and thy sons' wives with thee.

Genesis 9:9 And I, behold, I establish my covenant with you, and with your seed after you;

Genesis 9:11 And I will establish my covenant with you; neither shall all flesh be cut off any more by the waters of a flood; neither shall there any more be a flood to destroy the earth.

Genesis 9:17 And God said unto Noah, This is the token of the covenant, which I have established between me and all flesh that is upon the earth.

Genesis 17:7 And I will establish my covenant between me and thee and thy seed after thee in their generations for an everlasting covenant, to be a God unto thee, and to thy seed after thee.

Genesis 17:19 And God said, Sarah thy wife shall bear thee a son indeed; and thou shalt call his name Isaac: and I will establish my covenant with him for an everlasting covenant, *and* with his seed after him.

Genesis 17:21  But my covenant will I establish with Isaac, which Sarah shall bear unto thee at this set time in the next year.

Genesis 41:32  And for that the dream was doubled unto Pharaoh twice; it is because the thing is established by God, and God will shortly bring it to pass.

## EXODUS

Exodus 6:4  And I have also established my covenant with them, to give them the land of Canaan, the land of their pilgrimage, wherein they were strangers.

Exodus 15:17  Thou shalt bring them in, and plant them in the mountain of thine inheritance, in the place, O LORD, which thou hast made for thee to dwell in, in the Sanctuary, O Lord, which thy hands have established.

## LEVITICUS

Leviticus 25:30  And if it be not redeemed within the space of a full year, then the house that is in the walled city shall be established for ever to him that bought it throughout his generations: it shall not go out in the jubilee.

Leviticus 26:9  For I will have respect unto you, and make you fruitful, and multiply you, and establish my covenant with you.

## NUMBERS

Numbers 30:13  Every vow, and every binding oath to afflict the soul, her husband may establish it, or her husband may make it void.


## DEUTERONOMY

Deuteronomy 8:18  But thou shalt remember the LORD thy God: for it is he that giveth thee power to get wealth, that he may establish his covenant which he sware unto thy fathers, as it is this day.

Deuteronomy 19:15  One witness shall not rise up against a man for any iniquity, or for any sin, in any sin that he sinneth: at the mouth of two witnesses, or at the mouth of three witnesses, shall the matter be established.

Deutronomy 28:9  The LORD shall establish thee an holy people unto himself, as he hath sworn unto thee, if thou shalt keep the commandments of the LORD thy God, and walk in his ways.

Deuteronomy 29:13  That he may establish thee to day for a people unto himself, and that he may be unto thee a God, as he hath said unto thee, and as he hath sworn unto thy fathers, to Abraham, to Isaac, and to Jacob.

Deuteronomy 32:6  Do ye thus requite the LORD, O foolish people and unwise? is not he thy father that hath bought thee? hath he not made thee, and established thee?

# 1 SAMUEL

1Samuel 1:23  And Elkanah her husband said unto her, Do what seemeth thee good; tarry until thou have weaned him; only the LORD establish his word. So the woman abode, and gave her son suck until she weaned him.

1 Samuel 3:20  And all Israel from Dan even to Beersheba knew that Samuel was established to be a prophet of the LORD.

1 Samuel 13:13  And Samuel said to Saul, Thou hast done foolishly: thou hast not kept the commandment of the LORD thy God, which he commanded thee: for now would the LORD have established thy kingdom upon Israel for ever.

1 Samuel 20:31  For as long as the son of Jesse liveth upon the ground, thou shalt not be established, nor thy kingdom. Wherefore now send and fetch him unto me, for he shall surely die.

1 Samuel 24:20  And now, behold, I know well that thou shalt surely be king, and that the kingdom of Israel shall be established in thine hand.

# 2 SAMUEL

2 Samuel 5:12  And David perceived that the LORD had established him king over Israel, and that he had exalted his kingdom for his people Israel's sake.

2 Samuel 7:12  And when thy days be fulfilled, and thou shalt sleep with thy fathers, I will set up thy seed after thee, which shall proceed out of thy bowels, and I will establish his kingdom.

2 Samuel 7:13  He shall build an house for my name, and I will stablish the throne of his kingdom for ever.

2 Samuel 7:25  And now, O LORD God, the word that thou hast spoken concerning thy servant, and concerning his house, establish it for ever, and do as thou hast said.

2 Samuel 7:16  And thine house and thy kingdom shall be established for ever before thee: thy throne shall be established for ever.

2 Samuel 7:26  And let thy name be magnified for ever, saying, The LORD of hosts is the God over Israel: and let the house of thy servant David be established before thee.


## 1 KINGS

1 Kings 2:12  Then sat Solomon upon the throne of David his father; and his kingdom was established greatly.

1 Kings 2:24  Now therefore, as the LORD liveth, which hath established me, and set me on the throne of David my father, and who hath made me an house, as he promised, Adonijah shall be put to death this day.

1 Kings 2:45  And king Solomon shall be blessed, and the throne of David shall be established before the LORD for ever.

1 Kings 2:46  So the king commanded Benaiah the son of Jehoiada; which went out, and fell upon him, that he died. And the kingdom was established in the hand of Solomon.

1 Kings 9:5  Then I will establish the throne of thy kingdom upon Israel for ever, as I promised to David thy father, saying, There shall not fail thee a man upon the throne of Israel.

1 Kings 15:4  Nevertheless for David's sake did the LORD his God give him a lamp in Jerusalem, to set up his son after him, and to establish Jerusalem:

# 1 CHRONICLES

1 Chronicles 17:11  And it shall come to pass, when thy days be expired that thou must go to be with thy fathers, that I will raise up thy seed after thee, which shall be of thy sons; and I will establish his kingdom.

1 Chronicles 17:12  He shall build me an house, and I will stablish his throne for ever.

1 Chronicles 17:14  But I will settle him in mine house and in my kingdom for ever: and his throne shall be established for evermore.

1 Chronicles 17:23  Therefore now, LORD, let the thing that thou hast spoken concerning thy servant and concerning his house be established for ever, and do as thou hast said.

1 Chronicles 17:24  Let it even be established, that thy name may be magnified for ever, saying, The LORD of hosts is the God of Israel, even a God to Israel: and let the house of David thy servant be established before thee.

1 Chronicles 18:3  And David smote Hadarezer king of Zobah unto Hamath, as he went to stablish his dominion by the river Euphrates.

1 Chronicles 22:10  He shall build an house for my name; and he shall be my son, and I will be his father; and I will establish the throne of his kingdom over Israel for ever.

1 Chronicles 28:7  Moreover I will establish his kingdom for ever, if he be constant to do my commandments and my judgments, as at this day.

# 2 CHRONICLES

2 Chronicles 1:9  Now, O LORD God, let thy promise unto David my father be established: for thou hast made me king over a people like the dust of the earth in multitude.

2 Chronicles 9:8  Blessed be the LORD thy God, which delighted in thee to set thee on his throne, to be king for the LORD thy God: because thy God loved Israel, to establish them for ever, therefore made he thee king over them, to do judgment and justice.

2 Chronicles 7:18  Then will I stablish the throne of thy kingdom, according as I have covenanted with David thy father, saying, There shall not fail thee a man to be ruler in Israel.

2 Chronicles 12:1  And it came to pass, when Rehoboam had established the kingdom, and had strengthened himself, he forsook the law of the LORD, and all Israel with him.

2 Chronicles 20:20  And they rose early in the morning, and went forth into the wilderness of Tekoa: and as they went forth, Jehoshaphat stood and said, Hear me, O Judah, and ye inhabitants of Jerusalem; Believe in the LORD your God, so shall ye be established; believe his prophets, so shall ye prosper.

2 Chronicles 25:3  Now it came to pass, when the kingdom was established to him, that he slew his servants that had killed the king his father.

2 Chronicles 30:5  So they established a decree to make proclamation throughout all Israel, from Beersheba even to Dan, that they should come to keep the passover unto the LORD God of Israel at Jerusalem: for they had not done it of a long time in such sort as it was written.

## ESTHER

Esther 9:21  To stablish this among them, that they should keep the fourteenth day of the month Adar, and the fifteenth day of the same, yearly,

## JOB

Job 21:8  Their seed is established in their sight with them, and their offspring before their eyes.

Job 22:28  Thou shalt also decree a thing, and it shall be established unto thee: and the light shall shine upon thy ways.

Job 36:7  He withdraweth not his eyes from the righteous: but with kings are they on the throne; yea, he doth establish them for ever, and they are exalted.

# PSALMS

Psalms 7:9  Oh let the wickedness of the wicked come to an end; but establish the just: for the righteous God trieth the hearts and reins.

Psalms 24:2  For he hath founded it upon the seas, and established it upon the floods.

Psalms 40:2  He brought me up also out of an horrible pit, out of the miry clay, and set my feet upon a rock, and established my goings.

Psalms 48:8  As we have heard, so have we seen in the city of the LORD of hosts, in the city of our God: God will establish it for ever. Selah.

Psalms 78:5  For he established a testimony in Jacob, and appointed a law in Israel, which he commanded our fathers, that they should make them known to their children:

Psalms 78:69  And he built his sanctuary like high palaces, like the earth which he hath established for ever.

Psalms 87:5  And of Zion it shall be said, This and that man was born in her: and the highest himself shall establish her.

Psalms 89:2  For I have said, Mercy shall be built up for ever: thy faithfulness shalt thou establish in the very heavens.

Psalms 89:4  Thy seed will I establish for ever, and build up thy throne to all generations. Selah.

Psalms 89:21  With whom my hand shall be established: mine arm also shall strengthen him.

Psalms 89:37  It shall be established for ever as the moon, and as a faithful witness in heaven. Selah.

Psalms 90:17  And let the beauty of the LORD our God be upon us: and establish thou the work of our hands upon us; yea, the work of our hands establish thou it.

Psalms 93:2  Thy throne is established of old: thou art from everlasting.

Psalms 96:10  Say among the heathen that the LORD reigneth: the world also shall be established that it shall not be moved: he shall judge the people righteously.

Psalms 99:4  The king's strength also loveth judgment; thou dost establish equity, thou executest judgment and righteousness in Jacob.

Psalms 102:28  The children of thy servants shall continue, and their seed shall be established before thee.

Psalms 112:8  His heart is established, he shall not be afraid, until he see his desire upon his enemies.

Psalms 119:38  Stablish thy word unto thy servant, who is devoted to thy fear.

Psalms 119:90  Thy faithfulness is unto all generations: thou hast established the earth, and it abideth.

Psalms 140:11  Let not an evil speaker be established in the earth: evil shall hunt the violent man to overthrow him.


## PROVERBS

Proverbs 3:19  The LORD by wisdom hath founded the earth; by understanding hath he established the heavens.

Proverbs 4:26  Ponder the path of thy feet, and let all thy ways be established.

Proverbs 8:28  When he established the clouds above: when he strengthened the fountains of the deep:

Proverbs 12:3  A man shall not be established by wickedness: but the root of the righteous shall not be moved.

Proverbs 12:19  The lip of truth shall be established for ever: but a lying tongue is but for a moment.

Proverbs 15:22  Without counsel purposes are disappointed: but in the multitude of counsellors they are established.

Proverbs 15:25  The LORD will destroy the house of the proud: but he will establish the border of the widow.

Proverbs 16:3  Commit thy works unto the LORD, and thy thoughts shall be established.

Proverbs 16:12  It is an abomination to kings to commit wickedness: for the throne is established by righteousness.

Proverbs 20:18  Every purpose is established by counsel: and with good advice make war.

Proverbs 24:3  Through wisdom is an house builded; and by understanding it is established:

Proverbs 25:5  Take away the wicked from before the king, and his throne shall be established in righteousness.

Proverbs 29:14  The king that faithfully judgeth the poor, his throne shall be established for ever.

Proverbs 30:4  Who hath ascended up into heaven, or descended? who hath gathered the wind in his fists? who hath bound the waters in a garment? who hath established all the ends of the earth? what is his name, and what is his son's name, if thou canst tell?

# ISAIAH

Isaiah 2:2  And it shall come to pass in the last days, that the mountain of the LORD'S house shall be established in the top of the mountains, and shall be exalted above the hills; and all nations shall flow unto it.

Isaiah 7:9  And the head of Ephraim is Samaria, and the head of Samaria is Remaliah's son. If ye will not believe, surely ye shall not be established.

Isaiah 9:7  Of the increase of his government and peace there shall be no end, upon the throne of David, and upon his kingdom, to order it, and to establish it with judgment and with justice from henceforth even for ever. The zeal of the LORD of hosts will perform this.

Isaiah 16:5  And in mercy shall the throne be established: and he shall sit upon it in truth in the tabernacle of David, judging, and seeking judgment, and hasting righteousness.

Isaiah 45:18  For thus saith the LORD that created the heavens; God himself that formed the earth and made it; he hath established it, he created it not in vain, he formed it to be inhabited: I am the LORD; and there is none else.

Isaiah 49:8  Thus saith the LORD, In an acceptable time have I heard thee, and in a day of salvation have I helped thee: and I will preserve thee, and give thee for a covenant of the people, to establish the earth, to cause to inherit the desolate heritages;

Isaiah 54:14  In righteousness shalt thou be established: thou shalt be far from oppression; for thou shalt not fear: and from terror; for it shall not come near thee.

Isaiah 62:7  And give him no rest, till he establish, and till he make Jerusalem a praise in the earth.

# JEREMIAH

Jeremiah 10:12  He hath made the earth by his power, he hath established the world by his wisdom, and hath stretched out the heavens by his discretion.

Jeremiah 30:20  Their children also shall be as aforetime, and their congregation shall be established before me, and I will punish all that oppress them.

Jeremiah 33:2  Thus saith the LORD the maker thereof, the LORD that formed it, to establish it; the LORD is his name;

Jeremiah 51:15  He hath made the earth by his power, he hath established the world by his wisdom, and hath stretched out the heaven by his understanding.

## Ezekiel

Ezekiel 16:60  Nevertheless I will remember my covenant with thee in the days of thy youth, and I will establish unto thee an everlasting covenant.

Ezekiel 16:62  And I will establish my covenant with thee; and thou shalt know that I am the LORD:


# DANIEL

Daniel 4:36  At the same time my reason returned unto me; and for the glory of my kingdom, mine honour and brightness returned unto me; and my counsellors and my lords sought unto me; and I was established in my kingdom, and excellent majesty was added unto me.

Daniel 6:7  All the presidents of the kingdom, the governors, and the princes, the counsellors, and the captains, have consulted together to establish a royal statute, and to make a firm decree, that whosoever shall ask a petition of any God or man for thirty days, save of thee, O king, he shall be cast into the den of lions.

Daniel 6:8  Now, O king, establish the decree, and sign the writing, that it be not changed, according to the law of the Medes and Persians, which altereth not.

Daniel 11:14  And in those times there shall many stand up against the king of the south: also the robbers of thy people shall exalt themselves to establish the vision; but they shall fall.

## AMOS

Amos 5:15  Hate the evil, and love the good, and establish judgment in the gate: it may be that the LORD God of hosts will be gracious unto the remnant of Joseph.

## MICAH

Micah 4:1  But in the last days it shall come to pass, that the mountain of the house of the LORD shall be established in the top of the mountains, and it shall be exalted above the hills; and people shall flow unto it.

## HABAKKUK

Habakkuk 1:12  Art thou not from everlasting, O LORD my God, mine Holy One? we shall not die. O LORD, thou hast ordained them for judgment; and, O mighty God, thou hast established them for correction.

## ZECHARIAH

Zechariah 5:11  And he said unto me, To build it an house in the land of Shinar: and it shall be established, and set there upon her own base.

# NEW
# TESTAMENT

## MATTHEW

Matthew 18:16  But if he will not hear thee, then take with thee one or two more, that in the mouth of two or three witnesses every word may be established.

## ACTS

Acts 16:5  And so were the churches established in the faith, and increased in number daily.

## ROMANS

Romans 1:11  For I long to see you, that I may impart unto you some spiritual gift, to the end ye may be established;

Romans 3:31  Do we then make void the law through faith? God forbid: yea, we establish the law.

Romans 10:3  For they being ignorant of God's righteousness, and going about to establish their own righteousness, have not submitted themselves unto the righteousness of God.

Romans 16:25  Now to him that is of power to stablish you according to my gospel, and the preaching of Jesus Christ, according to the revelation of the mystery, which was kept secret since the world began,

## 2 CORINTHIANS

2 Corinthians 13:1  This is the third time I am coming to you. In the mouth of two or three witnesses shall every word be established.

## 1 THESSALONIANS

1 Thessalonians 3:2  And sent Timotheus, our brother, and minister of God, and our fellowlabourer in the gospel of Christ, to establish you, and to comfort you concerning your faith:

1 Thessalonians 3:13  To the end he may stablish your hearts unblameable in holiness before God, even our Father, at the coming of our Lord Jesus Christ with all his saints.

## 2 THESSALONIANS

2 Thessalonians 2:17  Comfort your hearts, and stablish you in every good word and work.

2 Thessalonians 3:3  But the Lord is faithful, who shall stablish you, and keep you from evil.

## HEBREWS

Hebrews 8:6  But now hath he obtained a more excellent ministry, by how much also he is the mediator of a better covenant, which was established upon better promises.

Hebrews 10:9  Then said he, Lo, I come to do thy will, O God. He taketh away the first, that he may establish the second.

Hebrews 13:9  Be not carried about with divers and strange doctrines. For it is a good thing that the heart be established with grace; not with meats, which have not profited them that have been occupied therein.

## JAMES

James 5:8  Be ye also patient; stablish your hearts: for the coming of the Lord draweth nigh.

## 1 PETER

1 Peter 5:10  But the God of all grace, who hath called us unto his eternal glory by Christ Jesus, after that ye have suffered a while, make you perfect, stablish, strengthen, settle you.

## 2 PETER

2 Peter 1:12  Wherefore I will not be negligent to put you always in remembrance of these things, though ye know them, and be established in the present truth.

www.ingramcontent.com/pod-product-compliance
Lightning Source LLC
Chambersburg PA
CBHW070751050426
42449CB00010B/2421